# SETTLEMENTS

# Settlements

## DAVID SUTTON

PETERLOO POETS

First published in 1991
by Peterloo Poets
2 Kelly Gardens, Calstock, Cornwall PL18 9SA, U.K.

**A catalogue record for this book is available
from the British Library**

**ISBN 1–871471–18–4**

Printed in Great Britain by
Latimer Trend & Company Ltd, Plymouth

**ACKNOWLEDGEMENTS** are due to the editors of the following journals and anthologies: *Poetry Review*, *Poetry Matters*, *Acumen*, *Home and Away* (Thamesdown/Southern Arts) and *An Enormous Yes* (Peterloo Poets) in whose pages some of these poems first appeared.

Supported by

Cornwall
County Council

WITH THE ASSISTANCE OF

SOUTH WEST ARTS

Recipient of an Arts Council Incentive Funding Award

For my daughter Elizabeth

# Contents

## Map-maker

There ought to be a survey done, with maps.
One shouldn't come upon them unawares.
I mean the places where you fall through time.
You know them by a lifting of the hairs,
A sudden tense alertness, not quite fear,
The air's electric whisper: *who goes here?*

It happens anywhere: an old canal,
The corner of a field, a cobbled mews.
I'd plot them all, a pointillist of time.
I've worked it out, the colours that I'd use:
Vermilion for the present, shading back.
The past's autumnal spectra end in black.

My maps would be a handbook for the haunted.
There'd be blood-red, then, for the motorways
With cities in their web like scarlet spiders,
But over here, in delicate flint-greys,
High on the downs pure Neolithic time
In chalky hollows, lingering like rime.

For furthest back, before the glaciers,
I'd let sloe-purple paint the night of caves.
My Roman ghosts would rise in blues and ochres
And Bronze Age russet glint about old graves.
How lovingly I'd chart one valley's scene
In Saxon gold and fresh mediaeval green.

But there's no school for time's cartographers
And any skill of mine to mark and keep
I'd lavish on the contours of the living.
It's only sometimes, at the edge of sleep,
I watch imagined colours pulse and fade.
How beautiful, the maps I never made.

## Scents

Tonight the rain in summer dark
Releases scents of leaf and bark:
The fumy reek of resined trees
And currant's sweet acridities.

Those aromatic compounds fit
Some membranous receptive pit
And trigger in my waiting brain
The memory of other rain.

I learnt my seasons from no class:
My summers were wild rose and grass,
A velveted and honeyed air.
Tonight I know: the past is there

And lies, so little does it need
To live again, in bush and weed
A yard or two beyond my door.
I am the child I was before.

Odours of earth, like love they came
Before the word, before the name.
The gates of time swing wide for these
Primaeval analeptic keys.

Then let me keep, though all depart,
These strange familiars from my start:
As in my first, in my last air,
Most potent molecules, be there.

# *Night*

Night is another country, like the past.
     I study there,
Learning how small a light will do at last:
     A muffled moon, one star,
How puddles in the blackest winter night
     Will spread a blacker glimmer, how the frost
Will lantern leaf and twig with haloed light
     To guide the lost.

I've watched, a darker shadow from the shade,
     Five badgers pass
Like broken moonlight moving in the glade;
     I've come on deer at grass
And fled with them the blind assaults of cars
     Like flash-floods in the gully of the lane
And waited till the only light was stars
     And seen again.

The unlit land is in me: when the towns
     Are loud with day
I close my eyes: a night-wind from the downs
     Has cleared the mist away.
The god I make myself is deep and still,
     Absorbing all, an endless starry dark.
I hear the train far off behind the hill,
     The farm dogs bark.

## For Beth

Dearest arrival, what a time to come.
Just when the party was over, never a doubt,
For children change, my love, they must go out
From the haven of our help, tall sons become
Voyagers: that's it, never again,
I thought, that trust, that sweet enquiring talk.
Families grow, like petals on a stalk.
Time is a wind that plucks. A gentle pain:
The years, I called it, nothing to regret.
We never thought, or dared, to ask for more,
Yet now you come, a small one, to our shore,
Time's compensation, our last gift and debt.
Sleep then, my daughter, on this guarded strand.
None ever came more welcome to my land.

## Settlements

In those days you were always moving on
To the place that didn't need you, to the town
With its milling squares and grey aloof cathedral
Or the village where the memories went down
So deep the conversations of the old
Were roots of willow threading time's black mould.

And the places took no note of you, or smiled
Seeing you come, intent on reverence,
But then retired, to business or stillness,
Behind the stone facade, the pinewood fence.
Where can the young belong? What can they own?
You travelled onward, unaddressed, alone.

Yet sometimes you would stop beside the road
In a place that was no place at all, you'd say —
One shuttered shop, a forecourt hazed with petrol,
The heat and silence of a summer day —
And voices would be round you, conjuring
The gift of something you alone could bring.

Or on the upland maybe, in a field
Where history had never been at all
You'd stop to shelter from a burst of rain,
Crouched in the nettled angle of a wall,
And feel about you, like a beating heart,
The dispossessed, unwilling to depart.

And you would stop your ears, and turn away:
Was this the heritage for which you came,
The edge of things, the spare, the unobserved,
All that had lost, or never knew, its name?
Somewhere another kingdom lay in wait.
You hurried on towards your true estate.

You are older now. You have your own domain,
A narrow land, but country of your choice.
It blurs a little, known so long, so well,
But not the other. Clearer now the voice
Of all that sought you, heavier the debt
You cannot pay, or own to, or forget.

# *Widow*

Twelve years alone. I watch time hunt you down.
Each meeting now, another earth is stopped:
Some building gone you knew from long ago,
Another friend to visit, lying propped
On death-ward pillows. What I do, I know —
The Sunday calls, the lunches in the town —
Weighs in the balance lighter than a leaf
Against the steady boulder of your grief.

I listen to the worries of the old:
The forms they send you, buses that don't run,
The closing shops, the tradesmen that won't call —
The genteel expectations one by one
Fall from you life. I listen to it all.
I counsel: have your comforts, don't get cold,
As if what tracked you were not sure and slow
And colder than a winterfull of snow.

Another place, another century
There might have been a solace for your kind:
The corner by the fire, the gathered children,
A life, to be recounted and refined.
They would have honoured you, that otherwhen:
Curator of the tribe, great mother-tree,
The rooted one with ripeness on her bough.
Your tribe is scattered: who will honour now?

We part. Again you tell me not to come
If roads are bad, if I've too much to do.
I reassure. I drive off in the dawn.
'You've got your job to get to.' Yes, that's true.
The pulpy silence of the winter lawn
Will start to beat within you like a drum.
I've left you something: cups to clear away.
You'll read the paper, wash up, face the day.

## In the Playground

A small one bumped his knee.
Another came to see,
A girl, with no defence
But clumsy innocence
Against another's pain.
She tried and tried again
To make his crying stop
By pirouette and hop:
'Look what I can do.
Now I've hurt myself too!'

The small one stopped and laughed
And she too, at her craft;
But then became aware
Of someone watching there
And blushed, as if for shame
That he should see her game
Who might not understand.
She took the small one's hand
And they were gone, unknown
Like fish beneath a stone.

# *Place-names*

"The place-names all hazed over
With flowering grasses ..."
                        Philip Larkin, "MCMXIV"

They are worn and durable
        As silvered oak,
The old names: Coombe and Barton,
        Stow and Stoke,

Burying the land
        Leaf-litter deep,
Gorgeous as Arundel
        Or plain as Steep.

Improbable on signs
        The past remains:
A Norman lorded here,
        There died the Danes.

That dyke the Saxons dug,
        This river-name
Murmured its light sound
        When Caesar came.

Bless the namers, men
        Of pen or plough.
History, receive
        Another now.

Poet, labourer,
        They do not pass.
We scent them on the map
        Like new-mown grass.

# On the Motorway

Lonely on the motorway, the light
Fading fast and eighty miles to go,
I conjure ghosts to travel with tonight
And see you there, your cigarette aglow,
No different for fourteen years of death,
And neither of us wholly at our ease,
As if we went to speak, but held our breath,
The way it always was. At last, to please,
'Nice car' you say. I shrug, indifferent.
You know we've judged life otherwise again,
But now for once I see your good intent
And what it overlies, the hidden pain.
We never talked. I know you wanted to.
I drew my silent pentacle around.
It would have hurt too much to let love through.
Too late, I'd ask you in now to my ground.
'I never understood . . . ' A silent touch.
The darkness turns. 'Was it like this for you:
That all you did seemed never to be much,
But what you did was all that you could do?'
You nod. 'I'm sorry.' 'Don't be. Children learn.
You think love's ever wasted?' Something bright.
The cigarette is gone, next time I turn.
I travel on, alone again, through night.

# The Anger of the Loving

The loving should not anger.
    They know the price of rage:
The mind upon a tether,
    The heart within a cage.

*And if it were tomorrow*
    *The end of love's delight,*
*That time should bring a sorrow*
    *To stretch the minutes tight?*

The loving should not anger
    Nor lie apart in pride
Like hills across a water
    Though side by touching side.

All pride and domination
    Are folly of the weak,
And still we let time tauten
    And only silence speak.

## Relatively Speaking

If we could have time slower
    Our longing might arrest
And keep the lightning's flower
    Dendritic, silver, pressed
On night's black slate forever,
    But love is dispossessed.

If we could have time faster,
    Our knowledge by such speed
Might have the coming chapter
    And all time's book to read
Till starlight's tale is over,
    But time will pay no heed.

Since no art yet can alter
    That enigmatic rate,
Upon a steady river
    We travel, yet await,
And understand time's answer
    Too soon, or else too late.

# At the Production Seminar

Coffee and biscuits, then the lecturer
On scheduling techniques: resources, shifts,
Heuristic algorithms, process times,
And I take notes, and later on will weave
A web beyond the dreams of Daedalus,
An electronic gossamer surveillance,
To lay upon men's labour, for the game
Is Mammon's mill, is productivity.

Look, we have slides: a grainy photograph,
Some factory at dawn. A worker stands
Under the striplights, blanched, anonymous.
What are you making, unit of production?
In bombs and bicycles, men take their pride.
What dreams defend you in this place, what love
Will you return to, when the sky's slow clock
Outside these windows wheels to darkening?

How fortunate, these human symmetries:
That man should be the animal he is,
So acquiescent in self-cancellation,
Selling his life so readily to live.
How good, that his productive energies
Should be consumed by our concupiscence,
That all should balance for him, toil and need,
Interminable and insatiable.

Comrade in the dawn, what can be said?
I know that art and love, like surface currents,
Ride on these rich upwelling deeps, sustained
By unacknowledged, cold ecologies
Complex as lianas: what can I
Do for you, friend? But let the photograph
Be focussed: show, for one unscheduled instant,
Your face, your private, unproductive eyes.

## Vocabularies

Like stars, or swarming bees, or flocks of birds,
We think them hardly countable, our words.

Yet fifty thousand's all we use, it seems,
For truth and lies, reality and dreams.

Which puzzles me. The world's more things than that.
Do languages grow lean as lives grow fat?

Is so much absent from our brains and eyes?
What's lost, I say, when we economize?

There's too much difference we make the same.
All poets love the miracle of name

Yet mourn exactitudes they cannot state:
The single noun that might denominate

Their moods of quietness like falling snow,
Or yearn for lexicons they cannot know:

The speech of eagles, what the dolphins sing,
The glossolalia of leaves in spring . . .

Nothing, we dream, could bring us to content
But fifty million words for what we meant,

To fit whatever happened like a glove,
Redeeming lost pluralities of love,

Until we wake to truth, and see again
Unharvested, like leagues of sunset grain,

Outnumbering all stars and bees and birds,
The matchless universe beyond our words.

# *Haiku for a Lunar Eclipse (17/8/89)*

On the shining rim
What crimes do you foreshadow,
Fingerprint of Earth?

Look, an ice-cap grows:
The glaciers of darkness
Burying bright lands.

Inexorable arc—
Yet when were these night's colours?
Rose, viridian.

Come, dark ferryman:
Lightly on the shining eye
Earth lays its obol.

Where the lily was
A bronze rose has unfolded
In night's old garden.

Stillness above all:
The stars for lack of moonlight
Burn more steadily.

# The Maharajah's Well

I love this well, that stands among the trees,
Gorgeous-preposterous, like a bower-bird,
With its pillared dome, rising in brown and gold,
Topped by a burnished spike, like the twist of a turban,
With its shining elephants, and scroll of carp.

It was Ishree, Maharajah of Benares,
That wrote to Edward Reade, Lieutenant Governor,
Born is the Ipsden country, friend to Benares
Through years of famine and mutiny, missing always
A far-off hamlet lost among the beechwoods,

"Edward, that story you told me troubles me.
To think of a child being beaten for stealing water!"
(The melt of glaciers carved out our valleys;
Since then no stream's endured: the waters glug
And vanish through the fine white sieve of chalk).

"Ours is a dry land too. Let a well be sunk
For our friendship's sake, and the sake of your people at home."
And so it was done, in eighteen sixty three
By Wilder of Crowmarsh, a foot for each day of the year
Hand-dug through chalk and perilous shored-up gravel,

And the Maharajah paid, and Edward Reade
Bought land, appointed a keeper, raised an orchard,
And bonfires blazed in the Maharajah's honour
That none need trudge again, raw-handed with buckets,
To clay-lined ponds half-choked with weed and rush.


Now this is true: you can go and see for yourself,
Since virtue is always surprising, like an oasis,
For the Maharajah is dust on the thirsty plain
And Edward Reade came home and departed at last
Into the dry-leaved silence of the beechwoods,

And water was brought by pipe: the well was barred,
But the dome is there, by the road among the trees,
And the shaft remains: if they let a bucket down,
They could draw up water still from the aquifer,
It would tremble again in the light, it would quicken and quench.

## Paths

What country has such paths? Our maps are green,
Reticulated like an insect's wing.
I love those veins. I trace them, summoning
Salt-road, flint-road, holloway: each scene
Rises responsive to my finger's course
As dot and dash pulse out their living morse.

These are the roads that talk. No tarmac here
To gag time's voice. That rut, that blue-rubbed stone,
Those polished roots say footsteps not my own
From immemorial kept my paths clear.
I see that long procession, race on race,
Moving before me at time's proper pace.

I'd follow it: look for me, if you will,
On some brown pathway like a spit of sand
That lakes of bluebell lap on either hand
Or on the green road where it mounts the hill,
The drover's road: I'd like to fall asleep
In wind and sunlight, counting vanished sheep.

But mostly under beeches look for me
Or listen where my rustling feet would cross
The paths that moonlight knows beneath the moss.
My shadow will be sharp . . . How can this be
Denied to me: was I not all my days
A woodlander and keeper of the ways?

## Urban Grass

Last of the green companions, grass,
You stand at bay in nature's pass
With banners threadbare but unfurled
Against a steel and concrete world.

In strip and square, on dusty banks,
In trodden, flayed, polluted ranks,
On arid marl and burning clay
Your long resistance wears away.

What Sparta bred you, not to yield
One acre of the stricken field,
Though none lament, where you obeyed,
The stubborn, democratic blade?

Or does the wind bring news again
And is it told about the plain
In some ancestral singing home
Of fog and fescue, bent and brome?

I dreamed earth had its honour too
That lived, for all that we could do.
I walked saluting in the street
The armies that will not retreat.

## Survivor

What's lost each century? The one before.
He's ninety. Quieter, he says. More green.
I glimpse it through him like a closing door.

He calls with things: a book, a magazine.
Can't stop, he says. Sits down, deplores the news,
Drinks coffee, talks of countries that he's seen.

Pressed trousers, overcoat, black shiny shoes.
He brings the children gifts: a joke, a sweet.
They listen to him but the clothes amuse.

How could they comprehend the long retreat:
But in good order, like a Guards' brigade,
Acknowledging withdrawal, not defeat,

Though all the roads run seaward? He has stayed
Too long, he says, won't do; shakes hands; steps out
Stiffly; late, you'd think, for some parade.

## Beth's Room

The new room's finished. Standing at the door,
I show my infant daughter where she'll sleep:
No curtains yet, or carpet on the floor;
A smell of paint like apples; sun; a deep
Unpenetrated silence. Yours, I say,
Forever, or as long as children stay.

But what's a room, demands her wide-eyed stare.
Why, love, a piece of Outside we make In,
A complex annexation of the air,
The property of stars, till we begin
To fence a little space with wood and stone
From all the universe to be our own.

Or say that it's a vessel, like an ark,
We load with life, that loud menagerie,
That bears us through alternate light and dark,
Our place of trust, our island on the sea.
Here you will sit: your longing and your love
Will fly from this wide window, like a dove.

And so it waits, this threshold you must cross,
Your second (for the first was into life),
And other rooms await you, to my loss,
But far off yet are womanhood and wife.
How still you lie, to watch the sunlight fall
And our two shadows, mingled, on the wall.

## Against Geologies

Our seconds rain like shells of lime
To build great thicknesses of time:
We watch the secret moments fall
Anonymous beyond recall,
Since who will look for you and me
In those white beds of history?

But if they do, with prying pen
When all our now has turned to then,
Let them not think, because they find
Some particle we left behind,
They know the vanished sea above
That was our salt and sunlit love.

These words I leave for them to learn
Like lily's stem or print of fern
Are but our shadow in the stone
And all the rest is ours alone.
Then what a world of touch and talk
Shall lie compacted into chalk.

## Plural

It's birth begins it, our disunity:
From one to not-one, so we learn to count.
Fingered by the first mists of infinity
Two is a signpost where the numbers mount
Up past all eyried crags by Cantor's track
To what no mind can visit and come back.

Who was it though? What prophet, mage or king
Was first, the very first, to dare that land?
What thunders pealed, that day of reckoning
We took the integers from God's own hand,
That starry knowledge, heavier than stone,
And came down-mountain, plural and alone.

## The Puzzle

Granted that we have it, this recall,
That at some random needling of the brain,
A word, a scent, roses will bloom again,
The dead walk in the country of the skull,
The puzzle still remains, so often, why
Our minds select the things they do for these
Synaptic resurrections: why those trees,
That patch of grass, a gate, some drizzling sky,
The time and place forgotten? It's as though
Something within us shies from too much sense
And counters it with pure inconsequence,
And yet they seem like things that we should know:
From days, perhaps, when all we did was live
Rapt, irrelevant, unpurposive.

# The Difference

The odd thing is, they say
That no electron differs
In all the universe
From any other: Feynman
Wrote, not quite in play,
That there might be just one
Primordial, immortal
Electron-under-all.

The other odd thing is
That no two snowflakes ever,
Not here, not anywhere,
Are quite the same, electrons
Having so many dances
And making by their dance
A snowflake's symmetry,
The stars, and you and me.

Then beautiful our oneness
That shall not be destroyed,
Enduring in the void
For always, everywhere.
But oh, our difference:
That shall not come back ever,
Not here, not in Arcturus,
Nor all the universe.

# Hush-a-bye, Baby

All right, dear, I'll not risk bad dreams again
For our small daughter, singing her to sleep
With my sad ballads. Now Sir Patrick Spens
Can stay dry-shod; Queen Jane shall not cry out
For Good King Henry in her agony;
The channering worm shall chide no more; fair Janet
Must leave her true-love to the elf-queen's keeping,
And Arlen's wife will absolutely not
Be pinned right through the heart against the wall.
Henceforth, as you request, I shall confine myself,
Like any normal dad, to nursery rhymes:
Strange egg-shaped characters will smash themselves
Irreparably; ill-housed, harassed mothers
Whip hungry children; babies fall from trees;
Mice shall be maimed; sheep lost; arachnophobes
Fare badly; innocent domestics suffer
Sudden nasectomies, and at the end
We shall dance rosy-faced in a ring and drop dead with the plague.

In either case, outside the small lit bedroom
The glass shall weep with rain, the winds be howling
Their old, uncensorable savageries.
But you are right, of course: we should choose well
What songs we sing, to lull them for a while.

## My People

My people never tell their love:
    Love ends where revelations start.
They keep it tethered like a yacht
    On private waters of the heart.
Some evening on the twilit roads
    They slip their moorings and depart.

That narrow craft each mans alone
    And none that watch those sails unfold
May know what skies are borne away
    Slow-gathered in the silent hold,
Nor if, upon another shore,
    Love makes a landfall, and is told.

# Prognosis

The matchless reflex of the eye
    Must lose its speed, the wrist its skill,
And that attacking swordsman Time
    Move like a dancer for the kill.

How measured, how mesmeric-soft
    The footfalls of his sure advance.
No stop withstands, no counterthrust
    Can fault the logic of his stance,

And others, better men than you,
    The Brave, the quick of mind and feet,
Fell back before him to the wall
    That leaves no possible retreat.

No declaration then, no deed
    Shall nove the master of the bout,
Yet some, I hear, have troubled him
    With what might almost be a doubt,

As if, one instant at the end,
    The pure resistance that they made
Perplexed the cool ironic eye
    That studied them above the blade.

## Second Summer

That was the summer when you named the world.
I'd push you round the lanes or carry you,
Your small face eager, wanting to be told,
And me too anxious, sometimes, for your due:
I wanted so much for you, mountains, seas,
As if it weren't enough for anyone
What I could give: one village with its trees,
Its cooing doves, its verges hot with sun,
And all around it, fold on secret fold,
My watchful land, the silences of moss,
The meditations of an ancient loss.

What did I think imagination needs?
Were Edens never nondescript before
With tarry fence and yellow wayside weeds,
Or had I grown too tall for love's first door?
Ah, when I thought I took you by the hand
Who was it led the other one to see
By lane and bank the lost enchanted land
Forever in its wordless mystery,
And when you blew the clock of silver seeds
That says that time is always and the same
Which of us taught, which of us learned, the name?

# The Beech Tree

Ten years ago I lay in hospital,
Not ready for it, tense, unsociable,
Stopped, as I had not been since I was born.
There was a tree: I'd wake to it each dawn,
All seethe and glimmer by my window pane,
And through the hot days turn and turn again
To where that house stood open: there were rooms,
Stairs, translucent attics, raftered glooms;
I'd lie beneath the lifting silken eaves
And feel the sunlight on my skin of leaves
And when I slept, within me I kept furled
The web and lattice of a secret world.
Not easy for my kind, the stubborn odd,
To ask the ministry of man or god,
But this at intervals for these ten years
Has come back to my mind, sudden as tears,
As if I lay again, too taut to breathe,
Then heard beyond the glass the gentle seethe:
My green physician, waiting out the night
To labour at the alchemies of light.

## At the Funeral

Funerals of the old are for the old:
The young, even the middle-aged, intrude,
Stiff in their unpractised piety,
Distracted by oak poppyheads, by light
From stained glass windows blue as irises.
There may be grief, but they are grateful too
To simplifying death that has unpicked
This knot of care from their much-tangled lives.
It is the old that mourn without alloy,
That shoulder loss and lay it to its rest.

Who are they though, so lusty at the back
With lifted voice, needing no book of hymns,
The sad spruce women and the grey-haired men?
What is it that they stare at past the air?
Outside, in winter sunlight, all's revealed:
The cousins of her youth, friends, neighbours, come
To honour old acquintanceship; now lives
Like long-divided rivers meet again,
A swirling confluence of memory
Carries the dead one to the final sea.

How gently they exclude one. 'That would be
Before your time.' 'That's going back a bit.'
But always to such time they do go back:
To rationing, the Blitz, heroic toil,
The fields of childhood, legendary snows,
Shops, terraces long gone. I understand:
Each dying nerves a new resistance, firms
A final bond of shared exclusiveness.
This is a closing ranks: like pioneers
They man the dwindling circle of their days.

The January sunlight has turned cold.
The ceremony's over. They depart
Down unsafe streets to doors they must keep locked.
What they came to do is done: somewhere
A girl they knew is running over grass
In a green country, leaving them behind
To counters and containments, ritual
And stoic unsurprise, such as they use
Whose lives have fed on long adversity,
Who know betrayal, and will not betray.

## The Dreamers

At night the strong field of the mind
That keeps our single world defined
Relaxes: then in dreams we see
Like fruits upon the quantum tree
The endless worlds of parallel,
And we are interchanged a spell
To live by that strange picture-show
The lives our waking cannot know.

For there in that infinity
All things that could have been must be.
So nightly we explore the ways
Of time's enchanted mirror-maze.
There on the paths we did not take
We meet the friends we did not make,
Embracing beautiful regret,
Or wake in danger's deadly sweat.

But this the cosmic censors keep
Fast locked behind the doors of sleep
And minds that tauten to the light
Forget their nightmare and delight,
Not knowing in what bliss or pain
To worlds of morning once again
They wake, those others on the tree
Who dreamed that they were you or me.

# From the Train

From the train at dawn, on ploughland, frost
Blue-white in the shadow of a wood.
Oh, you again, of all moods soonest lost
And most elusive and least understood.
What should I call you? Vision? Empathy?
Elation's tunnel? Worm-hole of rejoicing?
Some bliss of childhood, reasonless and free,
The secret microcosms . . . What a thing
To have no name for, yet to live for, these
Curious contentments under all,
These moments of a planet: weathers, trees—
What dreams, what intimations, fern-seed small,
Are buried in our days, that we must find,
And recognise, and lose, and leave behind?

# Geomancies

Like a careful Chinese geomancer
I play the game: *where shall I build my house?*
As if my days and money left more choice
Than standard boxes, twenty to the acre.

Good omens, said that craft, were cradled mound
Within the long blue curve of dragon hills;
A southern upland, where the sunlight falls;
Let water be before you, trees behind,

But keep yourself from pathways that are straight
And shun the level plain, the naked rock
That loose the secret arrows of ill luck ...
O gentle masters of an antique art,

What would you answer now, when all crafts falter?
Where shall we make our dwelling and our path,
Afraid of the deep poisons in the earth,
The sickness in the wind, the death of water?

Sorrow in all lands, and grievous omens.
Great anger in the dragon of the hills,
And silent now the earth's green oracles
That will not speak again of innocence.

## Barna-Oddr

He figures briefly in a near-forgotten
Viking saga, bearer of history's
Saddest nickname, Barna-Oddr.

Which means "Babies" Odd, and was given him because
He objected to a game his companions had
Of tossing children up and catching them
On the points of spears.

No more is heard of him. It is not known
How often, if at all, his spoilsport will
Prevailed. Only one thing is certain:
There were never enough of his tall, dissentient kind,
But those there were should be remembered, who had
No words of caritas, no star, but only
Uncertain, dangerous imaginings,
Stirring in their brutish minds, that things
Were better otherwise; who stood and spoke
Their flat, sword-hilted 'No'.

# Naming the Moths

"You'd call me poet? Hardly, Sir,
Arms and the man I did not sing,
But once upon an August night
I named the Yellow Underwing.

"We found on language's great map
A little corner, left all blank.
Such handiwork, without a name!
(The Maiden's Blush has me to thank).

"How I recall that dew-damp eve
Of honeysuckle-scented June
When first upon the Silver Y
I set the summons of man's rune.

"I see them now, our haunts of old,
Our hedgerow banks, our woodland glades.
Like memory itself they flit,
My Early Thorns, my Angle Shades.

"And some, you say, would honour us?
Then, Sir, we are obliged to you,
But such was never our intent.
We did what seemed our own to do."

Swifts and Ushers, fold your wings
Softly on the moonlit land.
They who loved you best are gone
Walking somewhere, lamp in hand,

Seeking down eternal lanes
Moths the angels might have missed,
Proffering before the Throne
"Some Amendments to Your List".

Willow Beauty, Burnished Brass,
　　　China Mark and all the Plumes,
With the Footmen gather, dance
　　　Lightly now above these tombs.

## Pen-friend

(for Yang Liuhong)

A girl, a poet, writes to me from China
In quaint uncertain English: in Beijing
Is spring, the trees and grass begin to green,
But wind and sand too much, the sky is yellow.
In Beijing autumn is best season: then
The sky is blue, the Fragrant Hill is red,
The Red Leaves red, the mountain is like fire.

Not sure how much she'll understand, I write
In quaint uncertain English back: I say
Here in my country also it is spring,
We have blue flowers underneath grey trees,
The stars last night were bright, I do not know
What stars shine on her country, I am sorry
I cannot write in her own language back.

She sends me poems someone has translated.
Her dreams are white: white coral, moonlight, snow.
Soon, she says, she understand me better,
Then she translate me: I become Chinese.
This grows too strange for my imagining:
Whom shall I meet now, on what fire-red mountain,
Talk with, in what yellow, windy spring?

# Hedge

They felled the hedge today:
    Hawthorn, tree of twilight,
A green cliff, streaked each spring
    With waterfalls of white.

Now let the voles unlearn
    Their lanes of leaf and bough.
What musty dark will keep
    The hedgehog's secrets now?

And let the birds lament
    Their sanctuary and store,
The redwings that will come
    To the coral feasts no more.

What autumn now shall light
    Their flare-marked landing-strip?
Tonight the hurdling wind
    Forgets its rise and dip.

It is only the eye that stumbles
    At a step no longer there,
The ear that ransacks silence
    For the long surf of the air.

# Layman's Guide

Neutrinos simply opt out
And go their own sweet way,
Speeding lawlessly
Through traffic-lights of lead,
Pausing only to flash one another
That hopeful physicists
With road-blocks of cleaning fluid
Are lurking ahead.

The others grow confusing —
Hadrons, bosons, mesons —
An empery of demons
Aswarm, self-conjuring,
Yet choreographed like angels
Each with its mass and spin.
Oh, more than we can imagine
They dance on the point of a pin.

But best are gravitons:
They do not appear on our screens,
Will not mix with the flashy, uptight
Electromagnetic brigade.
They ask no one to be impressed
But quietly, out of sight,
Go on holding things together,
Or at any rate, doing their best.

## Heatwave

The world's less real on summer afternoons.
We walk in dazzle, wan as daylit ghosts.
The streets are white and foreign: in dim shops
Assistants idle, sheened like melting wax.
In offices, in schools, in hospitals
The hours are burning dunes, and far off yet
Oasis evening with its water-dreams,
Its shadows and its cool solidities.

The countryside's no better: mirages
Sizzle on the surfaces of lanes;
The larks vibrate in poplared distances;
Crops swelter in the fields, on crumbling banks
The soil lips back from blue-white teeth of flint.
All roads are longer: air lies honey-thick
Round farmyard gates; a solitary child
Puddles its naked foot in pavement tar.

Truth is, this is no season for us now:
Untalking and untouching, we endure
Like cattle on the hillside, till day's ebb
Sucks at the round-pooled shadows of the trees.
"For the young" we say, disturbed at light
So riotous and squandered, suited now
To cooler, more reflective husbandries:
Night, and the moonlight's pure economy.

## Doppelgänger

Old doppelgänger, image in the glass,
Appearing like a witness as I pass,
You startle me, return my rueful smile,
Then settle to a pool of pure attention.
How candid still you look, so free of guile
      Or comprehension.

And how reluctantly you testify,
Though made by law to meet my level eye.
Your gaze is—what? Propitiation? Shame?
As if you would embrace me, like a lover,
But cold between lies what I cannot name,
      Nor you discover.

## Envoi

Most grow out of it, but now for me
It looks as if it will not end till death.
Some stubborn spring is wound too tight inside me
That cramps my gut, denies my words my breath.

So, the foolish, daily fight goes on:
People avoided, kindnesses unspoken,
Little salvaged but the desperate pride
Of those who are always defeated but never broken.

Also a little knowledge: how the world
Treats us, the grotesque, the vulnerable:
Its laughter, or surprising charity.
It is for certain faces most of all

In street or shop, the gentle, the perceptive,
I make these words that I shall never say
To stand for how I hope I might have acted
Had others been as I, and I as they.

## She

She inhabits our furthest silences.
 Her coming is like thunder
In gathering, electric distances
 Or the freckle of first rain.
Sometimes, walking in the winter street,
 You breathe her promise, like a sharpened air.
Listen, she says, be watchful: we shall meet.
 No hint of when or where.

So little time, of all the time that's ours,
 With her; so long to wonder
Where is she now, amid the stumbling years,
 And will she come again?
But then to meet, and all be as before,
 To read the question in her changeless eyes:
Do you ask more? No, Lady, nothing more
 And nothing otherwise.

# Climbing to the Ridge

A little while, to climb the ridge again:
The body flowing, smooth, on reels of silk;
Wicks of cotton-grass in winter sun
Luminous; red moss; the soil's black butter
Salted with white sand.
                          A little while
To see through wind-gapped mist the fields below
Gleam like ocean shoals, the lake a spearhead
Barbed and tanged with light.
                          A little while
To lie back under white sky; hooded, sleep;
Wake from warm throb to the kiss of snow
And come down-mountain, careless, like a rock-fall.
To say: where does it go?

Beyond the edge of hearing curlews cry.
The pools, wind-shivered, wait for others now.
What is there here to mourn?

Your song is in the silence.
Your stone is on the cairn.